What Can You Do?

by Renée Carver
illustrated by Terry Widener

Scott Foresman
is an imprint of

PEARSON

They can stop and go.
See Dad and Clint
stop and go.

You can stop and go.
Stop and go in a truck!

They can mop a spot of mud.
See Dad and Clint
mop, mop, mop.

1477 | 9780328386475 | 1477

Location: Aisle 1-Shelf 2

GWCLM.1CUO

Title:	READING 2010 (AI5) INDEPENDENT READER GRADE K UNIT 3 WEEK 5 WHAT CAN YOU DO?
Cond:	Acceptable
User:	gwcl_tvance
Station:	ECOM621-02
Date:	2024-12-24 15:20:24 (UTC)
Account:	Goodwill Good Skills
Orig Loc:	Aisle 1-Shelf 2
mSKU:	GWCLM.1CUO
vSKU:	GWCLV.0328386472.A
Seq#:	1477
unit_id:	24443193
width:	0.06 in
rank:	

GWCLV.0328386472.A

delist unit# 24443193

xxxxx

You can mop a spot of mud.
Mop, mop, mop that spot!

They can sip and gulp.
See Dad and Clint
sip and gulp.

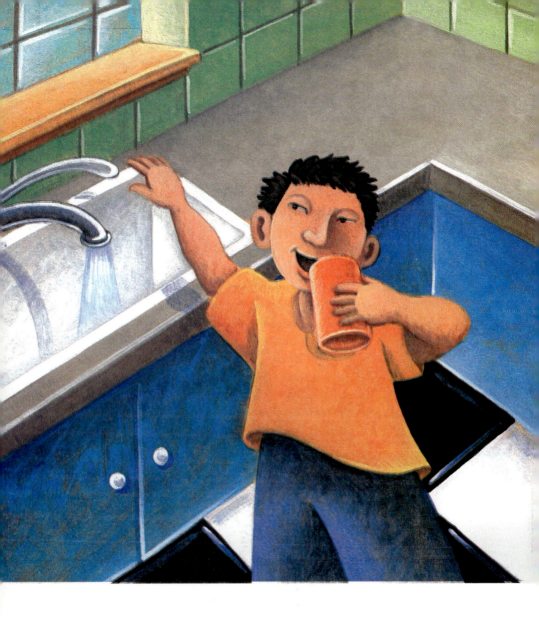

You can sip and gulp.
Sip, sip, sip!
Gulp, gulp, gulp!

They jump in the past.
You jump here.

Glenview, Illinois • Boston, Massachusetts • Mesa, Arizona
Shoreview, Minnesota • Upper Saddle River, New Jersey

Illustrations
Terry Widener

ISBN 13: 978-0-328-38647-5
ISBN 10:   0-328-38647-2

Copyright © Pearson Education, Inc. or its affiliate(s). All Rights Reserved.
Printed in the United States of America. This publication is protected by copyright and permission should be obtained from the publisher prior to any prohibited reproduction, storage in a retrieval system, or transmission in any form or by any means, electronic, mechanical, photocopying, recording, or otherwise. For information regarding permission(s), write to: Pearson School Rights and Permissions, One Lake Street, Upper Saddle River, New Jersey 07458.

Pearson and Scott Foresman are trademarks, in the U.S. and/or other countries, of Pearson Education, Inc. or its affiliate(s).

4 5 6 7 8 9 10 V0N4 17 16 15 14 13 12 11 10

Suggested levels for Guided Reading, DRA,™ Lexile,® and Reading Recovery™ are provided in the Pearson Scott Foresman Leveling Guide.

Scott Foresman Reading Street   K.3.5

Scott Foresman is an imprint of

ISBN-13: 978-0-328-38647-5
ISBN-10: 0-328-38647-2

ITZIK & MICKEY
Stories from Brooklyn & Beyond

*Irving Martin Glasser &
Myron Peretz Glazer*